Dear Aubrey.

This might take you back
a few year when you were a lad!
Love.
Len & Fred.
xxx.

FRANCIS FRITH'S

CHESHIRE

LIVING MEMORIES

DOROTHY NICOLLE was born in Uganda and later lived in Hong Kong. She was educated in Belfast and at Leicester University where she attained a degree in British Archaeology and History. She has also lived in the Middle East and in France. This gypsy life has encouraged a love of Britain and its history so that, these days, she knows that she has the perfect job - she is a Blue Badge Guide. She also lectures on various aspects of local and general history. Dorothy is married and now lives in Shropshire where she and her husband enjoy walking in the hills with their dogs.

FRANCIS FRITH'S
PHOTOGRAPHIC MEMORIES

CHESHIRE
LIVING MEMORIES

DOROTHY NICOLLE

First published in the United Kingdom in 2004 by
Frith Book Company Ltd

Paperback Edition 2004
ISBN 1-85937-675-4

British Library Cataloguing in Publication Data

Francis Frith's Cheshire Living Memories
Dorothy Nicolle

Frith Book Company Ltd
Frith's Barn, Teffont,
Salisbury, Wiltshire SP3 5QP
Tel: +44 (0) 1722 716 376
Email: info@francisfrith.co.uk
www.francisfrith.co.uk

Printed and bound in Great Britain

Front Cover: **CHESTER,** *Eastgate Street c1955* C82060
Frontispiece: **HATCHMERE,** *Lake Delamere c1960* H528019

*The colour-tinting is for illustrative purposes only, and is not intended
to be historically accurate*

AS WITH ANY HISTORICAL DATABASE THE FRITH ARCHIVE IS CONSTANTLY
BEING CORRECTED AND IMPROVED, AND THE PUBLISHERS WOULD
WELCOME INFORMATION ON OMISSIONS OR INACCURACIES

CONTENTS

FRANCIS FRITH: VICTORIAN PIONEER   7

CHESHIRE LIVING MEMORIES - AN INTRODUCTION   10

THE WIRRAL AND THE WEST   14

THE CHANGING BORDER ALONG THE NORTH   39

CENTRAL CHESHIRE   58

SOUTHERN CHESHIRE   81

EASTERN CHESHIRE   92

INDEX   115

Free Mounted Print Voucher   119

FRANCIS FRITH
VICTORIAN PIONEER

FRANCIS FRITH, founder of the world-famous photographic archive, was a complex and multi-talented man. A devout Quaker and a highly successful Victorian businessman, he was philosophical by nature and pioneering in outlook.

By 1855 he had already established a wholesale grocery business in Liverpool, and sold it for the astonishing sum of £200,000, which is the equivalent today of over £15,000,000. Now a very rich man, he was able to indulge his passion for travel. As a child he had pored over travel books written by early explorers, and his fancy and imagination had been stirred by family holidays to the sublime mountain regions of Wales and Scotland. 'What lands of spirit-stirring and enriching scenes and places!' he had written. He was to return to these scenes of grandeur in later years to 'recapture the thousands of vivid and tender memories', but with a different purpose. Now in his thirties, and captivated by the new science of photography, Frith set out on a series of pioneering journeys up the Nile and to the Near East that occupied him from 1856 unti 1860.

INTRIGUE AND EXPLORATION

These far-flung journeys were packed with intrigue and adventure. In his life story, written when he was sixty-three, Frith tells of being held captive by bandits, and of fighting 'an awful midnight battle to the very point of surrender with a deadly pack of hungry, wild dogs'. Wearing flowing Arab costume, Frith arrived at Akaba by camel sixty years before Lawrence of Arabia, where he encountered 'desert princes and rival sheikhs, blazing with jewel-hilted swords'.

He was the first photographer to venture beyond the sixth cataract of the Nile. Africa was still the mysterious 'Dark Continent', and Stanley and Livingstone's historic meeting was a decade into the future. The conditions for picture taking confound belief. He laboured for hours in his wicker dark-room in the sweltering heat of the desert, while the volatile chemicals fizzed dangerously in their trays. Back in London he exhibited his photographs and was 'rapturously cheered' by members of the Royal Society. His reputation as a photographer was made overnight.

VENTURE OF A LIFE-TIME

Characteristically, Frith quickly spotted the opportunity to create a new business as a specialist publisher of photographs. He lived in an era of immense and sometimes violent change. For the poor in the early part of Victoria's reign work was exhausting and the hours long, and people had precious little free time to enjoy themselves. Most people had no transport other than a cart or gig at their disposal, and rarely

travelled far beyond the boundaries of their own town or village. However, by the 1870s the railways had threaded their way across the country, and Bank Holidays and half-day Saturdays had been made obligatory by Act of Parliament. All of a sudden the working man and his family were able to enjoy days out and see a little more of the world.

With typical business acumen, Francis Frith foresaw that these new tourists would enjoy having souvenirs to commemorate their days out. In 1860 he married Mary Ann Rosling and set out on a new career: his aim was to photograph every city, town and village in Britain. For the next thirty years he travelled the country by train and by pony and trap, producing fine photographs of seaside resorts and beauty spots that were keenly bought by millions of Victorians. These prints were painstakingly pasted into family albums and pored over during the dark nights of winter, rekindling precious memories of summer excursions.

THE RISE OF FRITH & CO

Frith's studio was soon supplying retail shops all over the country. To meet the demand he gathered about him a small team of photographers, and published the work of independent artist-photographers of the calibre of Roger Fenton and Francis Bedford. In order to gain some understanding of the scale of Frith's business one only has to look at the catalogue issued by Frith & Co in 1886: it runs to some 670 pages, listing not only many thousands of views of the British Isles but also many photographs of most European countries, and China, Japan, the USA and Canada - note the sample page shown on page 9 from the hand-written Frith & Co ledgers recording the pictures. By 1890 Frith had created the greatest specialist photographic publishing company in the world, with over 2,000 sales outlets - more than the combined number that Boots and WH Smith have today! The picture on the next page shows the Frith & Co display board at Ingleton in the Yorkshire Dales (left of window). Beautifully constructed with a mahogany frame and gilt inserts, it could display up to a dozen local scenes.

POSTCARD BONANZA

The ever-popular holiday postcard we know today took many years to develop. In 1870 the Post Office issued the first plain cards, with a pre-printed stamp on one face. In 1894 they allowed other publishers' cards to be sent through the mail with an attached adhesive halfpenny stamp. Demand grew rapidly, and in 1895 a new size of postcard was permitted called the court card, but there was little room for illustration. In 1899, a year after Frith's death, a new card measuring 5.5 x 3.5 inches became the standard format, but it was not until 1902 that the divided back came into being, so that the address and message could be on one face and a full-size illustration on the other. Frith & Co were in the vanguard of postcard development: Frith's sons Eustace and Cyril continued their father's monumental task, expanding the number of views offered to the public and recording more and more places in Britain, as the coasts and countryside were opened up to mass travel.

Francis Frith had died in 1898 at his villa in Cannes, his great project still growing. The archive he created continued in business for another seventy years. By 1970 it contained over a third of a million pictures showing 7,000 British towns and villages.

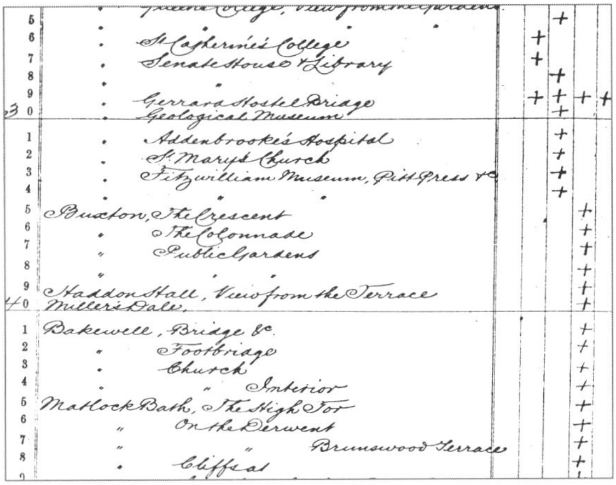

5 . Queens College, View from the Gardens
6 . St Catherine's College
7 . Senate House & Library
8 .
9 .
30 . Gerrard Hostel Bridge
. Geological Museum
1 . Addenbrooke's Hospital
2 . St Mary's Church
3 . Fitzwilliam Museum, Pitt Press &c
4 .
5 Buxton, The Crescent
6 . The Colonnade
7 " Public Gardens
8 "
9 Haddon Hall, View from the Terrace
40 Miller's Dale.
1 Bakewell, Bridge &c.
2 " Footbridge
3 . Church
4 . " Interior
5 Matlock Bath, The High Tor
6 " On the Derwent
7 " " Brunswood Terrace
8 . Cliffs at

FRANCIS FRITH'S LEGACY

Frith's legacy to us today is of immense significance and value, for the magnificent archive of evocative photographs he created provides a unique record of change in the cities, towns and villages throughout Britain over a century and more. Frith and his fellow studio photographers revisited locations many times down the years to update their views, compiling for us an enthralling and colourful pageant of British life and character.

We are fortunate that Frith was dedicated to recording the minutiae of everyday life. For it is this sheer wealth of visual data, the painstaking chronicle of changes in dress, transport, street layouts, buildings, housing, engineering and landscape that captivates us so much today. His remarkable images offer us a powerful link with the past and with the lives of our ancestors.

THE VALUE OF THE ARCHIVE TODAY

Computers have now made it possible for Frith's many thousands of images to be accessed almost instantly. Frith's images are increasingly used as visual resources, by social historians, by researchers into genealogy and ancestry, by architects and town planners, and by teachers involved in local history projects.

In addition, the archive offers every one of us an opportunity to examine the places where we and our families have lived and worked down the years. Highly successful in Frith's own era, the archive is now, a century and more on, entering a new phase of popularity. Historians consider the Francis Frith Collection to be of prime national importance. It is the only archive of its kind remaining in private ownership. Francis Frith's archive is now housed in an historic timber barn in the beautiful village of Teffont in Wiltshire. Its founder would not recognize the archive office as it is today. In place of the many thousands of dusty boxes containing glass plate negatives and an all-pervading odour of photographic chemicals, there are now ranks of computer screens. He would be amazed to watch his images travelling round the world at unimaginable speeds through internet lines.

The archive's future is both bright and exciting. Francis Frith, with his unshakeable belief in making photographs available to the greatest number of people, would undoubtedly approve of what is being done today with his lifetime's work. His photographs depicting our shared past are now bringing pleasure and enlightenment to millions around the world a century and more after his death.

CHESHIRE
AN INTRODUCTION

TO MANY PEOPLE who live in other parts of the country, Cheshire is simply 'that flat bit' of land that they pass through as they drive along the M6, somewhere between the built-up area around Birmingham and the built-up area around Manchester. In their haste to travel elsewhere, these people are ignoring a beautiful county that has so much to offer to visitors and residents alike.

'The air is very wholesome (so) that the people of the country are seldom infected with diseases or sickness … The people there live till they be very old; some are grand-fathers, their fathers yet living; and some be grand-fathers before they be married … The people of the country are of nature very gentle and courteous … they are stout and hardy; of stature tall and mighty … the women are very friendly and loving … and in all kind of house-wifery expert, fruitful in bearing of children, after they be married, and sometimes before'.

So wrote a visitor to Cheshire in 1656. The

BARNTON, *Nursery Road c1965* B518019

writer was obviously rather worried by the illegitimate state of many of Cheshire's children at the time, but apart from that, he paints a lovely picture of a county that is largely rural and prosperous. It has for a long time been a good place in which to live.

Indeed, to understand and appreciate Cheshire today you need to know a little about the Cheshire of the past. Much of it is low-lying land – I would hesitate to call it 'flat' – surrounded by the hills of Wales to the west and the Peak District on the east. The Cheshire Plain, as this region is known, provided good agricultural land, and would already have had a fair population by the time of the Roman invasion. The Romans, with their early ambitions for conquest of both Britannia and Hibernia, soon established a military post and seaport in Deva (today's Chester) overlooking the River Dee, and this was to become a vital link in their communications system in and around Britannia.

Later, new settlers arrived from the east; for all we know, they may have already been trading through Chester and known the port. Certainly they occupied the city, and the evidence of their success as settlers all around this area is to be found in the vast number of Anglo-Saxon place names in the county today. Later still, the River Dee was to prove an attractive entry point for Viking attackers; but the city survived, and was later to become a major port for all of medieval England.

In fact, throughout this period Chester was the main port on the north-western coast of England. However, from around 1400 the River Dee began to deposit silt around the city to such an extent that a new port had to be established at Shotwick. This, too, became silted up, so that Burton took over as Chester's port. It was succeeded in turn by Neston, then Parkgate, then Heswall, as 'the smothering sands' gradually covered all of the Dee estuary. Today, of course, it is Liverpool (once a tiny little fishing port by comparison) that is the dominant port hereabouts.

In those early days a large variety of goods would have been traded through Chester - wool, for example, and of course the famous Cheshire cheese. But there was another commodity that will have passed through the city: salt. This was a vitally important product from prehistoric times, so the silting up of the old ports must have been a disaster for salt producers, and may well have played a large part in the decision to canalise the River Weaver in the 18th century in order to reach ports along the Mersey.

Subsequently, the first proper purpose-built canal, the Bridgewater Canal, was developed; such was its success that before long it had been extended to link Manchester with Runcorn. So began the Canal Age, and soon canals were reaching almost all parts of the country. As their tentacles spread out, so the industries of the new Industrial Revolution quickly followed.

Before long cotton mills had been established on sites all along the canals. Some of these mills are to be found in places that strike us today as being far removed from the industrial heartlands of cities such as Manchester, in pretty little towns and villages like Marple and Bollington. It is often difficult to see them as former centres of industry. But everywhere the canal went, so industry seemed to go too.

With the 20th century, many industrial practices started to change. But the presence of salt under so much of Cheshire was still to play a large part in the county's economy, and new chemical industries were developed both in the heartland of the county around Northwich and Winsford and along the coast at places such as Runcorn and the enormous oil refinery at Stanlow.

Meantime, the railways of the 19th century and the motorways of the modern age also enabled people to move around more freely. This meant that people no longer had to live within the immediate vicinity of where they worked, and so rural communities that would otherwise have died were reinvigorated. This was to be particularly the case in the country to the south and east of Manchester. Those people who could afford to began to abandon the towns. This meant that fifty or so years ago, in the years immediately after the

Second World War, many of our towns were looking towards years of decline. This was the period during which the photographs collected here were taken. This sense of decline is not really reflected in these pictures; but then Frith's photographers were producing postcards for sale, and were unaware of the importance their pictures would later have in reflecting an aspect of the country that has now passed us by.

Fortunately, recent investment in many towns has seen a revival. This began in the 1960s with the development of Runcorn, for example, which had new expressways built all around it along with new shopping and residential centres. This trend has continued into more recent years, so

ELLESMERE PORT, *The Shropshire Union Canal c1955* E135010

12

that towns such as Warrington have become vibrant new centres for all types of business.

But in recent years, the main changes that have taken place in Cheshire have been changes to its borders. In fact, historically, borders have always had a strong influence on the development of this county. In Saxon times, when England was split into several different kingdoms, the River Mersey formed the border between Mercia and Northumbria. Later, when these kingdoms were split into shires or counties, Chester's shire (or Cheshire) was formed, with the river still defining its northern boundary. Meantime, King Offa has already defined the western boundary of his realm of Mercia by building Offa's Dyke, and this was to become the basis of a sinuous boundary separating England from Wales. As a result, Chester was to play an important military role in keeping the peace and controlling this border for centuries to come.

The county that had been formed in Saxon times was to last for over 1,000 years; then, with the 20th century came the growth of urban districts such as could never have been imagined all those years ago. As these massive urban sprawls developed, they ignored the early boundaries, so much so that their administration became extremely unwieldy. And so, to the disgust of many people, a nationwide reorganisation of county, or rather administrative, boundaries took place in 1974. Several of these new administrative regions (I hesitate to call them counties in the old sense) were formed locally – Wirral and Merseyside and Greater Manchester – and the old boundary of the River Mersey (whose name in Saxon times actually meant 'boundary river') was ignored. In the west, Birkenhead, at that time the largest town in Cheshire, was lost to the new region of Wirral. In the east, a far larger chunk of the county was taken away to become linked to Manchester, a city that, it must be admitted, had long since become the dominant influence in the lives of people who lived here.

But that does not make it any easier to accept the changes if you consider yourself to be a Cheshire man or woman. In fact, it is easy still to meet people who live in this region who will insist that 'the new boundary is a mile or so to the north of us here, we are in Cheshire' - such is the cachet that a Cheshire address has over one in Greater Manchester.

And how did those people who were proud to be Lancashire born and bred feel when they were told they now lived in Cheshire? For this was what happened to the districts around the towns of Widnes and Warrington, which were presumably given to Cheshire to make up for territories lost elsewhere. Many of them were not terribly happy either. Children being born in the region today will grow up never knowing anything else; but it will take much more than a single generation before old allegiances die away.

These recent changes have been reflected in the selection of many of the photographs in this book. There are a number of photographs that have been included that purists will notice were taken in areas that were not part of Cheshire at the time they were taken, or are not part of Cheshire as it is today. Their inclusion has been the result of a deliberate decision on my part to remind us of the changes made along this northern border.

THE WIRRAL AND THE WEST

BIRKENHEAD
Hamilton Square 1967 B399039

Birkenhead is no longer technically part of Cheshire.
From a small settlement in 1811 with 105 people, the
population of the 'City of the Future' had already risen
to 2,569 by 1831. It developed as a port for Chester as
other ports on the Wirral became silted up, but it was
always rivalled by Liverpool just across the Mersey.
It hardly deserves its other title of 'Liverpool's ugly little
sister', however.

BIRKENHEAD
The Crossroads 1954
B399006

The crossroads pictured here are on the Woodchurch Road near Prenton. The bank building sitting to the left of the junction has been totally remodelled for new offices, and now has a very smart glass-fronted upper storey. Notice the two men on their motorcycles waiting at the lights – neither is wearing a crash helmet, as these were not then compulsory.

BEBINGTON
St Andrew's Church c1955 B660027

There are two Bebingtons – Higher and Lower. These photographs were taken in Lower Bebington. Founded in Saxon times, the church we see now largely dates from around the 14th century; a local legend says that when ivy grows to the top of the spire the end of the world will be nigh. People here are careful to ensure that no ivy grows on the church.

BEBINGTON
The Village c1955 B660014

It has been said of Bebington that 'though the town centre is lacking in character, it is also open, green and wholesome', and that description still works well now. Most visitors to the town today are on their way to a place close by that has a great deal of character – the purpose-built town of Port Sunlight with its 'sylvan suburbs' around the nearby soap factory.

UPTON
The Village c1950
U45002

For a long time Upton was an important market centre in the north Wirral with its markets and fairs attracting people from far and wide, but today it has become a suburb of the much more important Birkenhead. Two pubs are shown on the left – the Eagle and Crown and behind it the Horse and Jockey. Both survive today, but the Horse and Jockey now occupies a new building around the corner.

18

UPTON
Arrowe Park Road c1950 U45009

Arrowe Park, just outside Upton, was once the home of John Ralph Shaw, a wealthy Liverpool warehouse owner. In 1929 the park was the site of the Scouts' World Jamboree, and over 50,000 scouts came here. Unfortunately they chose one of the wettest summers on record for their meeting, so that the Jamboree quickly became known as the 'Mudboree' instead.

HOYLAKE
The Yachts c1960
H277008

The waters around Hoylake are very shallow these days, so that it is difficult to believe that there was once an important deep-water anchorage here known as Hoyle Lake. Consequently the town served as a departure point for troops travelling to Ireland with King William in the 1600s prior to the Battle of the Boyne.

HOYLAKE, *The Railway Inn c1965* H277020

Today the size of this pub (built in 1938) reminds us that by the 20th century Hoylake had become a holiday resort. Even earlier it had been described as a place where you could 'find genteel society, good accommodation at reasonable prices, and one of the most commodious bathing-places' in England.

HOYLAKE
Market Street c1960
H277056

Today, those people outside Cheshire who have heard of Hoylake know it because of the Royal Liverpool Golf Club, which is situated to the west of the town. Golf is big business these days, so that it comes as no surprise to find that one of the shops here now has the name hoylakegolfcentre.com over its window.

HESWALL, *Telegraph Road c1955* H276053

For most people, the village of Heswall is centred on this road, the A540, linking Chester with all the towns along the western side of the Wirral. Here the road is lined with shops, including the rather picturesque row of shops, typical of its period, on the right here - it dates from 1936 and is called Castle Buildings.

HESWALL, *School Hill c1955* H276047

The original village, however, was at the bottom of the hill, centred on the church of St Peter, with the estuary of the Dee beyond. Notice the shop in the building on the right – this was known to local children as Dolly's Shop, and it served as an unofficial tuck shop for the local children from the school that was between it and the church below.

HESWALL
The Village c1955 H276068

It is a steep climb from the old village to the shops in the new area. Fortunately, for those who live at the bottom of the hill near the church there is another row of smaller shops, and many of them, including the post office shown here, still survive.

NESTON
The Cross c1960
N88021

It is interesting, through photographs such as these, to see how road traffic islands change - compare this with picture N88036 (below). Today the island around the drinking fountain is once again almost as small as it is in this photograph. The fountain itself is a memorial to a local man, Christopher Bushell, and dates from 1882.

NESTON
The Cross c1965
N88036

Despite its grand appearance, the tower shown here is really just a folly over the entrance to a house. Built of beautiful polished red Ruabon brick, and with lots of fine decorative detail on it, the local story is that it was erected simply to make this the tallest house in Neston! Opposite sits a pub, the Greenland Fishery, the only one of that name in the country.

PARKGATE
The Old Quay c1965
P255046

Burton, Neston and Parkgate were all once major ports. Each in turn became silted up, and trade eventually moved to Birkenhead and Liverpool. The Old Quay pub in Parkgate reminds us of this early history. For a time Parkgate was the main disembarkation point for travellers going to Ireland – Handel stayed here briefly in 1741 waiting for favourable winds to take his ship to Dublin.

PARKGATE
The Red Lion Inn c1960
P255031

'All on one side, like Parkgate' is a Cheshire saying which perfectly describes the way all the houses along the Parade look towards the sea. Today the sand banks are a haven for bird life – 'What is the Dee estuary, if not a place for birds? … They come here in their thousands … The only thing that comes near to outnumbering them are the birdwatchers'.

BURTON
The Village c1955
B561020

It is difficult to believe that this sleepy little village was once a bustling seaport – there were five alehouses along this street some 400 years ago! But there is no pub here now. Today Burton is a conservation area; in fact, the village has to be one of the most attractive in the county.

BURTON
Barn End c1955
B561034

It is houses like this that make Burton so attractive. The Bible tells us that we should build our houses on rock and not sand – and all the oldest cottages in Burton sit perched on outcrops of sandstone. Barn End is a timber-framed cruck house (made from trees split and shaped to form the frame for both wall and roof of a building) and is thought to be the oldest in the village.

PUDDINGTON, *The Village c1955* P268001

It was once said of the village that 'Puddington is singularly quiet; it is so quiet that it has never yet reached the fame of a picture postcard'. This photograph shows that Frith's postcard company, at least, reached the village. It also reminds us of how much can change, since the row of houses shown here have all gone, to be replaced by some bungalows.

WILLASTON
The Village c1965
W371042

On the other hand, the main street of Willaston has changed very little. Notice Aston's (right) – it is still there. In the 1960s this was a haberdashery, run by the Aston family for two generations. Today the name survives, but it is now a tea shop.

WILLASTON
The Green c1965 W371052

This is a scene that we seldom come across these days – a traffic jam caused by a lorry meeting a herd of cows walking to, or perhaps from, their milking parlour. The pub is the Nag's Head Inn. Traditionally pubs of this name were places where you could hire a horse; such animals would obviously be 'nags', as no-one would hire out good quality horses to all and sundry.

HOOTON
The Church c1960
H363003

Designed by James Colling, St Paul's Church was built in 1852-62. It is extremely fanciful for some tastes, using three different stones (two red and one white) to give a pattern of bands of colour all around the building. The church cost £5,000; it was paid for by a Liverpool banker, R C Naylor, and his wife. Naylor had previously bought the Hall at Hooton, but this was demolished in 1922 .

ELLESMERE PORT, *The Shropshire Union Canal c1955* E135010

The town owes its very existence to the building of the Ellesmere Canal (as it was then called) by Thomas Telford and William Jessop in the 1790s. This linked the Mersey ports with industrial centres in the heart of England. Today the Boat Museum in the dock area reminds us of the way of life of those early boatmen and their families.

ELLESMERE PORT
Dock Street c1955
E135022

This is a most fascinating photograph, because the entire row of buildings on the left of the road has gone – the M53 motorway now runs right through their old back yards. Just one or two buildings on the right survive to confirm where we are, including the Horse and Jockey pub.

MOLLINGTON, *The Mollington Banastre Hotel c1965* M239005

The hotel takes its name from the local village name and that of Robert de Banastre, who acquired the estate in the 12th century. The old manor house on the site was replaced by the present building in 1853. Converted first of all into a country club, it became a hotel in 1964.

CHESTER
Eastgate Street c1955
C82060

This photograph gives an excellent view of the top of one of the stairways leading to Chester's famous Rows (in the bottom right corner of the photograph). Unique to the city of Chester, the Rows are a double tier of shops that are thought to date back to medieval times.

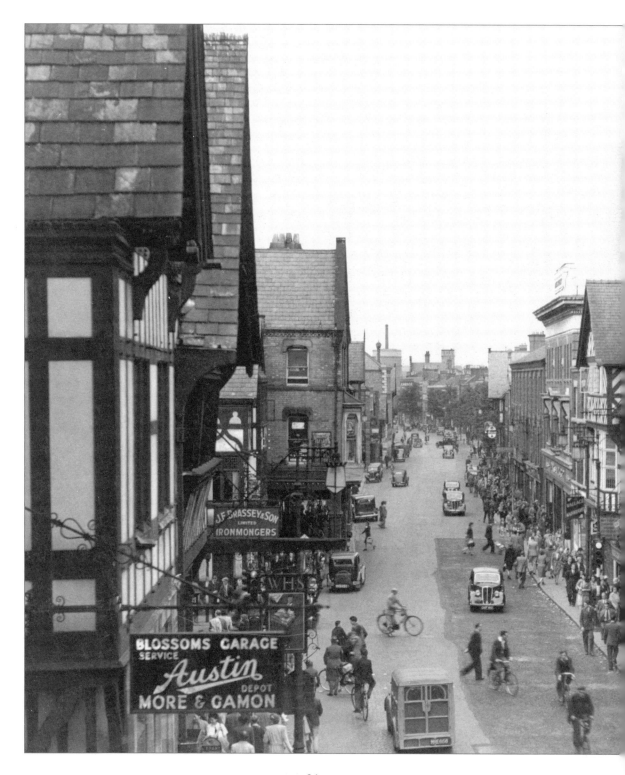

CHESTER
Foregate Street c1955
C82065

The heart of the present-day city of Chester sits right on top of the old Roman town of Deva. The walls around that town still survive, and this is the view looking beyond those old city walls to the east – the photographer was standing right over the old gate. The word 'foregate' means the 'area before the gate'.

35

CHESTER ZOO
Molly the Elephant
c1955 C768024

Chester Zoo was founded in 1934, and a number of animals were brought here for safety during the Second World War, including Molly. She was looked after by an Indian mahout, and in those days, before the zoo had the proper boundary fences that it has today, he was regularly to be seen taking Molly for walks in the surrounding area.

CHESTER
The Zoo, Jimmy the Orang-utan c1960
C768113

It was in the years following the war that Chester Zoo acquired the excellent reputation that it has today for its breeding programmes, including the breeding of orang-utans. Jimmy, pictured here, was the first to arrive. He came in 1958, and before long had acquired a reputation amongst the staff as an escapee, always managing to get away from the island where he was housed.

ECCLESTON, *The Pump and the Post Office c1955* E17002

Pretty though the village is, it has no pub. Apparently there was one here once – until one Sunday the Duke of Westminster, within whose estate the village lies, was passing by after a church service. He saw all the villagers sitting outside drinking when, he thought, they should have been in church. So he closed it – the pub, that is!

ECCLESTON
The Ferry c1965 E17007

This was a particularly popular haunt during late Victorian and Edwardian times - in those days there was a rope ferry across the River Dee. The ferry was a family-run business operated, to begin with, by a ferryman called 'Jimmy the Boat', and later by his descendents. Today, even the motor-powered ferry has gone.

FARNDON, *The Bridge and Holt c1955* F161004

We are looking from Farndon towards the bridge crossing over the English-Welsh border marked by the River Dee, with Holt (in Wales) beyond. The bridge is said to be haunted by the spirits of two young Welsh princes whose bodies were thrown into the river from here:

'Belated travellers quake with fear,

And spur their starting horse,

For childish shrieks, they say they hear

As Farndon's Bridge they cross.'

THE CHANGING BORDER ALONG THE NORTH

WIDNES, *Victoria Square c1950* W97012

One of the new towns acquired by Cheshire following the border change in 1974, Widnes developed in the 1800s along with the new chemical industries. These were not at all regulated at first, so that the air here was particularly foul – in 1862 the Alkali Act was passed to ensure stricter control of the conditions under which people worked. Typical of many new Victorian churches is St Paul's, shown here (left), which was built in 1883.

WIDNES
*The Runcorn-Widnes
Bridge c1965* W97026

Below the bridges we can
see the River Mersey,
which was the former
county boundary. At this
point the river crossing
narrows to form the
Runcorn Gap, so that there
was a ferry here from
medieval times. Compared
to the new road bridge
(left) the railway bridge on
the right seems so clumsy
– its foundations had to
be built under the water,
and go down some 45 feet
below the low-water mark.

WIDNES
The Municipal Buildings c1965
W97072

Widnes was once described as 'the ugliest and most depressing town in England', and perhaps this building helps to explain why. Recently, however, there has been considerable investment in rejuvenating and developing the town, so much so that apparently property prices in and around the town are now rising faster here than in almost any other part of the country.

RUNCORN, *The Two Bridges c1955* R67032

This is a fascinating photograph, because it shows both the railway bridge (built in 1868; it even had a pedestrian walkway along it) and the transporter bridge in front. The latter was constructed in 1905, and was one of only three of its type in the country. In its first year it carried 187,000 passengers. It was decommissioned in 1961 when the new bridge was opened.

RUNCORN
Widnes Bridge c1965
R67049

Quite simply, this bridge is stunning when the sun shines on it. Opened in 1961, it was then the third largest bridge in the world, and it had the largest steel arch in Europe. It was later enlarged to carry six lanes of traffic, and was then renamed the Silver Jubilee Bridge in 1977 to commemorate the Queen's Jubilee.

ASTON-BY-SUTTON
The Church c1955
A360002

This is a delightful little church in a very peaceful setting to the south of Runcorn. The chancel dates from 1697; it was built by Sir Willoughby Aston, who was apparently very influenced by Vanbrugh. The nave, with its large windows letting in plenty of light for the congregation, dates from 1736.

DARESBURY, *The Parish Church c1955* D151001

Most famous as the church where Charles Dodgson (better known as Lewis Carroll) was baptised in 1832, the church now has a memorial window with scenes from the Alice books, and draws visitors from all over the world. Lewis Carroll's father was the vicar here; unfortunately, the parsonage in which Carroll was born was destroyed by fire in 1883.

MOORE
The Post Office c1955 M240003

Once poor moorland (hence the name of the village), the land locally was all drained when first the Bridgewater and then the Manchester Ship Canals were built on either side of this 'pleasant backwater'. The post office pictured here is now a private house. The signs on the wall advertise *The Listener*, *Woman* magazine and the *Radio Times*, amongst others.

HIGHER WALTON
Walton Church c1955 H526089

Although its style is medieval, this church, dedicated to St John the Evangelist, was built in 1885 by Sir Gilbert Greenall, a Lancashire MP and founder of the famous brewing company that bears his name. There is a window in the church that shows St George, but the face of the saint is that of a descendent of Sir Gilbert's who died in 1928.

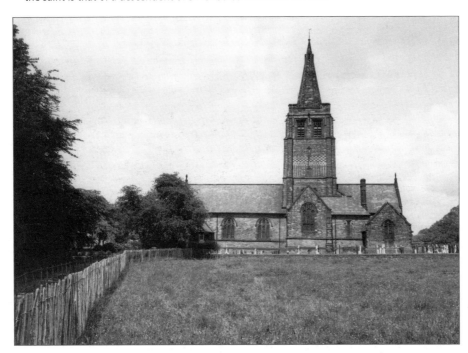

HIGHER WALTON
Walton Hall c1955
H526026

Walton Hall was largely built in 1836-38, although additions date to 1870. It was sold (along with its extensive land) to the Warrington Corporation in 1941 in order to pay death duties. By then dry rot had been discovered, so that one wing of the building was demolished. The grounds are now open to the public, and include a golf course.

WARRINGTON
Bridge Street c1950
W29037

We have crossed the Mersey once more, and are back in what was once Lancashire. Although all the main buildings remain the same, the centre of Warrington has totally changed in the last twenty or so years. Much of this development would have happened anyway, but there has also been a determination on the part of the local people to deliberately rebuild for a better future following the tragedy caused by an IRA bomb here.

WARRINGTON
The Town Centre from Boots Corner c1950 W29025

Prosperity came to Warrington along with industry in the 1800s, and this is reflected in the quality of all the town's commercial buildings. The variety of industries here was enormous – from glass making to the production of pins, tanning, sailcloth and soap production, brewing and, inevitably in this area, chemical industries.

WARRINGTON
Horse Market and Town Centre c1950 W29009

All of this area of Warrington has now been pedestrianised. Just behind the 'Keep Left' road sign there is a shop called The Fifty Shilling Tailor (left); a suit for fifty shillings would be excellent value – that translates as £2.50. Mind you, fifty shillings bought considerably more then than £2.50 would today.

WARRINGTON
Ye Olde Barley Mow
c1955 W29058

It is a surprise to discover this pub surviving in the market in Golden Square, surrounded as it is by Georgian, Victorian and later buildings. The Barley Mow dates from 1561, and it has the most wonderfully ornate façade. Warrington's market, incidentally, is one of the largest in the northwest, and has over 250 stalls.

WINWICK, *The Church c1960* W370003

St Oswald's Church sits on a slight rise. A local legend says that the people planned to build it on lower land, but each night, after work, a pig came along and moved all the stones back up to the top of the hill. They therefore understood that they were being told to build on the hill, and that is why the church is there. A carving of a pig on the building reminds us of the story.

WOOLSTON
Holes Lane Corner c1955
W415010

The title of this photograph places this scene in Woolston, but the shop on the left calls itself Paddington Post Office. Woolston and Paddington are two of the many small villages and hamlets that have been absorbed as Warrington has grown. These shops now sit overlooking a dual carriageway on what was once the main road linking Warrington with Manchester.

WOOLSTON, *The Secondary Modern School c1955* W415001

This school may have been quite new when this photograph was taken, but it does look so uninspiring. Fortunately, although the building has hardly changed at all in the intervening years, the school, now known as Woolston High School, looks a much more welcoming environment in which to study these days.

GRAPPENHALL
Church Street c1955
G200010

Two pubs and a church – some would call that a perfect combination. The Ram's Head is in the foreground, with the Parr Arms just behind.
The church is dedicated to St Wilfrid, and local legend has it that this is where the Cheshire cat originated – there is a carving of a cat on the tower. Some say it was the signature of a man called Catterall who worked on the church.

THELWALL
The Pickering Arms c1955
T328003

Thelwall has claimed to be England's smallest city – the title dates from Saxon times. Like Moore, it is sandwiched between two canals. When the large Manchester Ship Canal was built, a ferry service was offered to the local people, and the fare, originally one old penny, was fixed by Parliament. Today there is still a ferry crossing to the Eyes, now a bird sanctuary.

GRAPPENHALL, *The Canal c1955* G200014

Winding around the village is the Bridgewater Canal. Cut between 1759 and 1765, it was the first canal built in England and, along with the Industrial Revolution, which was then also taking place, it was to change the world. In this area the canal was used for the transportation of fustian, a form of rough cotton known as 'poor man's velvet' that was produced locally.

LYMM
The Canal c1960 L122026

Here we have another view of the Bridgewater Canal, this time in Lymm. After the Second World War, the use of canals around England for the transportation of industrial goods almost completely ended. However, enlargement of this photograph shows that the boat pictured here is carrying coal. Fortunately, the pleasure boat industry for holidaymakers has since revived the canals and saved them from total dilapidation.

HIGH LEGH, *The School c1955* H362003

The village of High Legh probably gets its name because it was an early settlement in a forest clearing sitting on high land. The name was then taken by the two main families that owned land here – the Leghs and the Leighs. No longer a primary school, the building pictured has now been converted to serve as the local village hall.

KNUTSFORD
The Royal George Hotel, King Street c1955 K47017

The people of Knutsford will tell you that this town's name comes about because there was a ford here for King Canute. The Royal George Hotel, an old coaching inn, is the building in the centre. Despite signs depicting King George III, it was actually called the George and Dragon until 1832, when Princess Victoria (later Queen Victoria) visited – it then acquired the epithet 'royal'.

KNUTSFORD
King Street c1955
K47012

Knutsford was home for many years for the writer Elizabeth Gaskell. Her novel *Cranford* was published in 1853, and gives a delightful picture of town life in mid 19th-century England. In 1985 a Gaskell Society was founded, and it now has around 500 members from all over the world.

MOBBERLEY
The Victory Hall and New Road c1955
M238008

This is an attractive, relatively undeveloped little village. It has a station linking it to Manchester, so many people who live here work in the city. Consequently it is surprising that it has not been developed more – until you learn that it sits on great underground salt beds, and a fear that these might subside is all that holds the developers back!

MOBBERLEY
The Cricket Ground
c1955 M238012

Victory Hall (shown in picture M238008 on p.53) serves as the village hall, and was built to commemorate the First World War – hence its name. Just behind it is the cricket club, founded in 1876. It must be difficult to play here sometimes on busy summer weekends – the ground lies very close to the end of the runway of Manchester's airport.

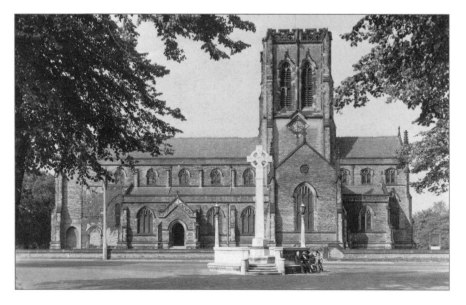

DUNHAM MASSEY
St Margaret's Church
c1955 D155002

St Margaret's sits halfway between Altrincham and the estate of Dunham Massey (now maintained by the National Trust), hence the title given by Frith's to this photograph. The church was built in 1855. Originally there was a spire on top of that powerful tower, but this was removed in 1927. The war memorial has also been moved – it now sits well within a memorial garden across the road.

ALTRINCHAM, *The Old Market Place c1955* A40024

In today's world the advertisement on the lorry in the centre of the picture would be considered terribly politically incorrect. It shows a young Indian boy wearing a turban and holding a packet of Black Boy tea! Otherwise, apart from the vehicles and a few coats of paint, this scene has changed little in the last fifty years.

ALTRINCHAM
Stamford New Road c1955
A40011

'Altrincham has a town centre without any attraction and is trying to do something about it.' So said Nikolaus Pevsner when he described the town. The clock tower in the distance sits outside the town's railway station – the railway came to Altrincham in 1849, after which the town rapidly developed as a suburb to Manchester.

SALE
Wash Way Road c1960
S344032

The A56 linking Altrincham with Manchester is a road lined almost the entire way with houses and shops. They all date largely from that time between the two World Wars when the motor car became king; the buildings shown here are typical of the period. The cinema behind the trees is now a fitness centre.

SALE, *The Town Hall c1955* S344002

'Sale has a bit of a centre by the town hall and little else.' The Town Hall, designed by C T Adshead, was opened in 1915, with an extension added in 1940. It sits right beside the canal, an area that has seen a great deal of development recently with old warehouses being converted for modern use, so perhaps that description is a little unfair.

SALE

Northenden Road c1965 S344025

Mind you, only a short walk from the town hall (seen here in the distance) and we are in parts of the town that can only be described now as having seen better days. Perhaps the redevelopment around the Town Hall will soon have an effect here too.

CENTRAL CHESHIRE

HELSBY, *The Rock c1955* H326003

Helsby's name means the 'village on a ledge', but it would be more correct to say that it nestles just under the ledge or outcrop of rock seen here. It is said locally that 'as long as Helsby wears a hood (meaning this protective ledge I assume), the weather's never very good'. At 464 feet above sea level the tor has a commanding position, and was used by the Celts as the site for an early hill-fort.

HELSBY
The BI Works and Sports Ground c1955
H326006

For a long time the main industry here was cable making. This began in 1887 with what was then the Telegraph Manufacturing Company. It later became British Insulated Callender's Cables Ltd, which is the name on the long low building to the left of the chimney. BICC is no longer here, but the white building remains – it is the Helsby Sports and Social Club.

FRODSHAM, *From the Hill c1955* F176009

Taken from Overton Hill, this view shows the town with the Mersey estuary in the distance beyond the sand dunes. It is from here that the Sandstone Trail now begins. This runs for 30 miles through the heart of Cheshire, and ends by the locks of Grindley Brook just on the border with Shropshire.

FRODSHAM
High Street c1955
F176019

Although the road narrows as it climbs the slope, the main street of Frodsham, from where this picture was taken, is said to be one of the widest such roads in England. This was an important route linking Chester with Runcorn and the north, and the large pub on the left, the Bear's Paw, reflects this. It dates from 1632, but was restored 'rather to its detriment' in the early 1900s.

HATCHMERE
The Woodfield Café, Blakemere Lane c1960
H528013

Now called the Delamere Forest Inn, the pub sits close to what remains of the Delamere Forest. This was a medieval hunting forest, and once extended from Frodsham all the way almost to Nantwich. It was officially disafforested in 1812, when some land was reserved for what is now the Forestry Commission.

HATCHMERE, *Lake Delamere c1960* H528019

Today, after considerable localised replanting, there are over 2,000 acres of woodland in the vicinity, through which wander numerous walking and cycling trails all centred on Lake Delamere. There is also an excellent Forest Centre with a small exhibition area describing the local fauna and flora.

HATCHMERE
The Forest Café c1955
H528034

Enlargement of the photograph reveals the signboards with the various Sunday papers vying for your custom with such enticing lures as 'The world of the formerly married', 'Ulysses – the inside story of the film', '1,000 hours of Hell' and, best of all, perhaps, 'DEBS! The truth at last – by the man who knows'.

DELAMERE
The Fishpool Inn c1960
D153004

Delamere, originally called 'foresta de la mare', is a very scattered community with no real village centre. There was once a healing well somewhere in the forest which, legend has it, was blocked up during an invasion by Vikings. Then in 1600 a new well appeared which had miraculous properties, healing people who were blind, deaf or lame. Was it the same well? We will probably never know.

DELAMERE
The School c1960 D153006

Still a village school, this is the Delamere Church of England Primary School, with a little nursery in the building just beyond. The school was built in 1846, and is very large and ornate for a village school of the period.

LITTLE BUDWORTH
Oulton Park c1960 L310008

Oulton Park was once the setting for a beautiful house, built in 1716. Unfortunately, it burnt down in 1926, and during the fire six people were killed trying to save artworks from the building. During the Second World War American forces were stationed here, and it was they who built the roads that are now used for the racetrack - the site was taken over for motor racing in 1953.

LITTLE BUDWORTH
Oulton Mill Pool c1960
L310011

This tranquil pool was dammed to supply water for a mill sited just behind the photographer. It lies within the old Delamere Forest, and nearby there is a small section of that original forest surviving – it is considered so important that it is now a Site of Special Scientific Interest, and is carefully managed to preserve it.

SANDIWAY, *Toll Bar c1960* S490038

Notice the early traffic lights (left). This is now a major (and very much busier) road junction for routes between Chester and Manchester and also between Warrington and the south. Sandiway is now permanently linked with Cuddington: the two villages were officially joined together in 1935.

WHITEGATE
Main Road c1965
W529039

Whitegate is named for an old white gate which would once have marked the entrance to the former Vale Royal Abbey. Today there is another white gate at the entrance to the church, just across the road from this delightful old cottage. Nearby there is a 5½-mile trail, the Whitegate Way, that follows an old railway line built in the 19th century to transport salt.

HARTFORD, *The Cross Roads c1955* H323018

Now really a suburb of Northwich, Hartford has long been a more desirable area in which to live, particularly in the past for the town's wealthier manufacturers. Its name comes about because it sits close to the River Weaver, where once, presumably, there was a fording point where deer would cross – a good spot for hunters (or poachers).

DAVENHAM
The War Memorial and the School c1955
D152001

This old school was built in the 1850s, but in recent years it has been converted into a number of separate private houses. This school may have closed down, but there are still a number of others in the area – an independent school, primary and secondary schools and two special-needs schools as well.

67

NORTHWICH
Witton Street c1960
N43050

'Northwych is a prati Market Towne, but fowle'. So wrote Leland in the 16th century. This is the most northerly of Cheshire's famous salt towns; today I would hesitate to call it pretty, but I certainly would not call it foul. The tall building on the left was the post office; although it looks a typical black and white building, it was actually built in 1911. Today it has been transformed into a pub – appropriately called the Penny Black.

NORTHWICH
Witton Street c1965
N43067

Because of the underground mining of salt, the town has suffered severely in recent years from the effects of subsidence, and now all new buildings have to be built with this in mind. One building lost to subsidence was the former library. Today's library is the timber building set back slightly on the right of the picture – it is the Brunner Library, and originally adjoined an old salt museum.

NORTHWICH, *Town Bridge c1960* N43032

This unusual bridge was both the first road swing bridge on floating pontoons in Britain (it was built in 1899) and then the first electrically operated swing bridge (in 1989). It was designed by Colonel J A Saner. It recently underwent restoration, including strengthening for today's far heavier traffic, in 1998.

WEAVERHAM
High Street c1955 W368002

Close to Northwich, Weaverham straddles an old Roman road, thus reminding us of the importance of the salt mines in this area nearly 2,000 years ago. In the 1930s an excavation in the local churchyard unearthed a mass grave in which many of the skulls had a single bullet hole in the forehead – this macabre discovery was dated to the Civil War period.

WEAVERHAM
Northwich Road c1965
W368035

The timber cottage on the left is Poplar Cottage, dating from the 1600s. It had a room on the ground floor that was traditionally a 'birth chamber'. The idea was that after its birth, when leaving the house, the newborn child would have to be carried upstairs – there is an old saying that in order to rise in the world you should first go up some stairs.

ACTON BRIDGE, *The River Weaver near Acton Swing Bridge c1955* A235011

Now used just for pleasure boating, the River Weaver would once have been very busy with boats carrying salt to ports along the Mersey estuary. There is a law (that has never been repealed) which states that 'to swim in the River Weaver on a Sunday is an offence punishable by deportation to the Colonies'.

BARNTON
Nursery Road c1965
B518019

Barnton is a small town with most inhabitants employed by the nearby chemical works at Winnington. It is said that the people of Barnton were once so poor that they could only afford to eat 'jam butties' - consequently the town came to be known as 'Jam Town'.

COMBERBACH, *The Spinner and Bergamot Inn c1955* C479011

The pub pictured here, the Spinner and Bergamot, was built in 1792, and is named after two racehorses. Enlargement of the sign in the photograph shows that 'Burgamot' is spelt with a 'u' rather than an 'e'. Burgamott was a kind of tapestry made from the hair of goats or oxen, so perhaps there is an old connection here with spinning and weaving.

GREAT BUDWORTH, *High Street c1965* G201008

Pevsner says of Great Budworth that it is 'one of the best pieces of villagescape in the county. Yet there is hardly a house that would need a close look'. There were once four pubs in Great Budworth – the White Hart, the Ring o'Bells, the Saracen's Head and the George and Dragon (left), the only one to survive. It has a particularly fine wrought iron sign.

LOWER PEOVER
The Church c1955 L308011

Despite the stone tower that the visitor sees first, it is the timberwork of St Oswald's Church that makes it so stunning. The early timberwork has not been accurately dated, but the church was founded in 1269. If this timberwork dates from that first church, as is thought possible, then this could well be one of the oldest arcaded wooden frame churches in Europe.

LOWER PEOVER
The Bells c1955
L308013

The pub is the building on the right. Notice the arms displayed between the windows - they have now been moved to the top of the gable wall. They are the arms of Warren de Tabley; the pub's official name is the de Tabley Arms. However, in 1871 the landlord was a man called George Bell, and since then the pub has been known as the Bells. George Bell is said to haunt the beer cellar.

ALLOSTOCK
All Ways Filling Station c1955 A213005

These old petrol pumps have long gone. In the 18th century there was a boys' school in Allostock run by a minister of the Unitarian chapel; it was attended at one time by Robert Clive, the future conqueror of India. Clive is said to have been thrown out of three schools – perhaps this was one of them!

GOOSTREY
The Primary School c1960
G199026

Today this is the annexe for Goostrey's primary school, which now occupies a larger site across the road. The tower of St Luke's Church rises just beyond (centre) – local legend states that a yew tree in the churchyard was used to make archers' bows in the Hundred Years War. Cheshire's bowmen were the best in England, and land here was granted to two archers in 1365 following the Battle of Poitiers.

HOLMES CHAPEL
The Church c1955
H519001

St Luke's Church would appear to be made of stone and brick, but in fact the main body of the church is timber, encased in brick outside and plaster within. This was done in the 18th century, and it is only recently that timbering in the ceiling has been rediscovered. Bullet marks on the lower part of the tower date from the period of the Civil War.

GOOSTREY
Station Road
c1960 G199023

When these pictures were taken, Goostrey had recently become home to 'Lovell's Saucer', the local name for Jodrell Bank. It was set up by Professor Bernard Lovell in 1956, and was then the largest radio telescope in the world. Not only is it important for scientists, but today there is also a planetarium to explain the heavens to ordinary visitors.

MIDDLEWICH, *The White Bear Hotel c1950* M237004

'Wych' was the Saxon term for saltworks, so Middlewich was therefore the middle one of Cheshire's three salt towns. In the days before refrigeration, salt was essential for the preserving of food. When the Romans established a town here they called it 'Salinae', meaning 'the saltworks'. Our word 'salary' comes from the Latin word for salt because Roman soldiers were often paid in this commodity.

MIDDLEWICH
King Street Schools
c1950 M237008

It was along the line of present-day King Street that the Roman saltworks, and therefore the Roman town, were based, together with a fort at the far end. Today this area is residential. The school building in the foreground has now been restored for use as a parish centre.

OVER, *Town Square c1965* O92036

'Ouver standeth on the east end of Delamere Forest … and is but a small thing': so ran a description in 1620. For all that it was created a borough in 1280, Over never really developed, and in 1894 it was described as 'the smallest municipality in the country'. Today it is really a part of the larger community of Winsford. 'Town Square' is something of a misnomer – this is just a roundabout beside the shops.

WHARTON
The Church c1955 W417001

Like Over on the other side, Wharton was once far more important than Winsford, but is now merely a part of that town. In fact Winsford only developed when the Weaver River was canalised in 1731. Some years later, when the Trent and Mersey Canal was being planned, it was deliberately cut through Middlewich and kept away from Winsford for fear of competition with the river.

WINSFORD
Fountain Court
c1965 W561046

Winsford underwent enormous change in the 1960s when a new road system was built through the town. This obliterated many old buildings and moved the heart of the town to an entirely new focus, the Winsford Cross Shopping Centre, pictured here. Enlargement of the photograph shows that the Co-op (centre) has a sign in its window advertising 'New Food Hall Now Open'.

WINSFORD
The War Memorial and the Schools
c1955 W561011

The new dual carriageway was built all along this length of road, but fortunately all these buildings survive. The school in the foreground dates from 1906, and beyond it, Brunner Guildhall and Verdin Grammar School both date from the 1890s. The latter is now used by the Mid Cheshire College. The war memorial, however, has been moved.

WINSFORD
General View c1960
W561033

This view shows the town before the changes of the 1960s had taken place. Winsford sits on beds of almost pure salt laid down around 200 million years ago. Mining has been carried out for centuries, and today salt is still extracted locally – it is the only working rock salt mine in Britain. The salt is used for gritting roads in icy weather or for the production of fertilisers.

WINSFORD, *The Flashes c1960* W561014

The salt mines underground are enormous, so large that miles and miles of road systems, big enough for double-decker buses, have been formed to travel around on; in fact there are 22 million cubic metres of nothing under the ground here. So perhaps it is no wonder that through history, these great holes have sometimes collapsed. Some of them subsequently filled with water to become lakes, locally called flashes.

SOUTHERN CHESHIRE

TARPORLEY, *The Swan c1965* T218079

The Swan was an important coaching inn in the past.
The present building dates from 1769, although it
contains within it parts of an earlier medieval building.
It is also the headquarters of the oldest hunting club in
England – the Tarporley Hunt – which predates the
hotel, as it was founded in 1762. The colonnaded area
just beyond is the former covered market.

TARPORLEY
High Street c1965
T218090

When this photograph is enlarged, it is possible to make out a sign for the Fire Station on the right. Founded in 1869, Tarporley's fire brigade was the first voluntary fire brigade in the country. The building was used to billet troops during the Second World War, and then as a labour exchange, before the fire brigade moved back in 1957. Today the building is home to a chocolate shop.

EATON
The Village c1955
E162043

Until around 1950 Eaton had twenty thatched buildings, but today only about a third of that number survives, including Hunter's Close pictured here. The plinth in the foreground was probably once the site of a medieval cross. Today there is a new cross here, erected in 1977 to commemorate the Queen's Silver Jubilee.

BEESTON, *The Castle c1955* B57054

The castle's name tells us that originally this marvellous hilltop site was somewhere where commerce took place. It has been a fortified site since Celtic times, although the castle whose ruins we see today dates from the 1200s, when it was one of a series of castles all along the English-Welsh border.

BEESTON
The Castle Entrance c1955
B57059

Although it had fallen into disrepair by the time of the Civil War, the castle was then refortified; it changed hands a couple of times during the war, and was finally slighted in 1645. It was taken over by the Ministry of Works (the ancestor of today's English Heritage) in 1959, and now has a very good little museum within the gatehouse area.

PECKFORTON, *The Elephant and Castle c1955* P722063

Despite the obvious assumption that this sculpture adorns a pub, there was never a pub of that name in this area. Instead the carving was in the garden of a cottage called, appropriately enough, The Elephant and Castle. It was carved in the mid 19th century and originally had a fine pair of tusks – they are broken in this photograph.

BUNBURY
The Crewe Arms Hotel c1960 B562012

Sitting on the southern side of Bunbury, the Crewe Arms has now
been renamed the Yew Tree at Bunbury. Photographs such as this
are a remarkable reminder of just how fast plants can grow,
because the buildings in the distance are now well hidden
behind tall trees.

NANTWICH
High Street c1965 N3065

Traditionally Nantwich was the most important of Cheshire's three salt towns, although salt production ceased here in the 1800s. The salt did bring great wealth to the town, however, and this is exemplified by many of the lovely black and white buildings such as the four-gabled building shown here, which dates from 1584.

WRENBURY
Oak House and the Church c1955
W414001

Despite a new dormer window and conservatory, Oak House is still instantly recognisable. But the view of the church from this spot is totally changed as a result of the trees and foliage planted alongside the hedge. The church of St Margaret dates from around 1500, and is especially noted for the 17th-century box pews that survive within.

NANTWICH, *The Shopping Centre c1965* N3072

Today's shopfronts have rather less individuality about them. The two sections of road here each (technically at least) have different street names: Swine Market is on the left and Oat Market on the right, reminding us of what used to be traded here in times past.

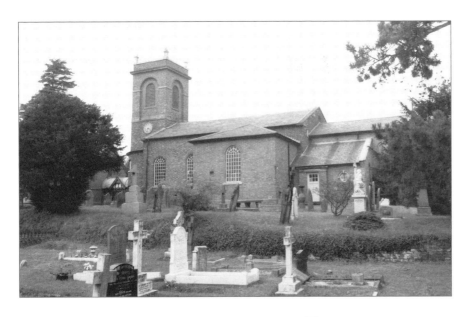

WISTASTON
St Mary's Church c1955
W502063

St Mary's Church was built in 1827-28 and was designed by George Latham, who lived in Nantwich. By the 1880s, following the development of nearby Crewe as a railway town, Wistaston had become a sizeable suburb, so the chancel was increased in length and the transept was added. A covered porch (just visible in the picture to the left of the tower) was added in 1905.

CHURCH MINSHULL
The Main Street c1955
C478012

This scene is almost totally different today - the position of the telephone kiosk (left) is about the only thing that tells us where we are in Church Minshull. The cottage just beyond the kiosk used to be occupied by the lady who ran the old telephone exchange for the village; today there is a purpose-built exchange building on that same site.

CREWE, *The Square c1955* C316023

The statue in the centre of the Square is the town's war memorial – Crewe was a new industrial town with a relatively youthful population, so that many of the town's men were called up to serve in both world wars. We are reminded of this fact when we consider the large number of men remembered on the plaques around the statue.

CREWE
Market Square c1960
C316056

The presence of four buses circling the Square in photograph No C316023 (p.88) is a reminder that that picture was taken before the nearby bus depot was opened in 1960. The depot is just to the right of the building with the clock tower, Big Bill as it is known locally.

CREWE, *Market Street c1955* C316031

This view shows the other end of the Square abutting Market Street. Marks & Spencer can just be seen on the left. Further along, across the road, enlargement of the photograph reveals a branch of Boots – Boots is still on this site today, but in a new shop that was built in the 1960s.

HASLINGTON, *The Village c1960* H324013

The white building (right) is the Hawk Inn in the centre of Haslington. It is now more obviously an old building, because the plaster has been removed to reveal the timber structure underneath – it is thought to date to 1510. The highwayman Dick Turpin is said to have stayed here once.

SANDBACH

The Saxon Crosses c1965
S489046

First recorded in 1565 as 'two square crosses on stone steps, with certain images and writing thereon graven', these superb crosses were destroyed by Puritans in the following century. Since then the broken pieces that survived have been gathered together and restored, insofar as was possible. The carving detail is quite remarkable.

SANDBACH
The Black Bear Inn and the Market Place c1955 S489009

Nikolaus Pevsner says of the Market Place that it 'is unusually attractive in that it retains its cobbles', and fortunately these are still here today. The Black Bear, on the left, dates from 1634, and is one of a number of pubs situated around the Market Square. Just beyond is the tower of St Mary's Church, which was largely restored in the 1840s by George Gilbert Scott.

ALSAGER
Sandbach Road c1960 A214011

The original part of the town of Alsager was to the north of here. The development of this part of the town only really dates from the opening of the railway between Crewe and Derby in 1848. Alsager's station is just where the road bends, and there is a level crossing at this point, just beyond the cyclists.

EASTERN CHESHIRE

HYDE
Market Street and the Town Hall c1950 H231003

Described by Pevsner as 'uninteresting', the Town Hall
was designed by J W Beaumont and built in 1883-85. The
clock and bells on the building were donated by Joshua
Bradley. The plaque that commemorates him states that
'it is better to be nobly remembered than nobly born', a
sentiment of great meaning in a town that played such
an important part in the Chartist movement.

HYDE
Market Street 1968
H231029

Another of Cheshire's cotton towns, Hyde was to be the scene of great industrial unrest when in 1848, a local group of Chartists marched through the town to disable the boilers, bringing all machinery in the mills to a standstill. The Chartists were so-called because they sought 'a charter of rights for all' with both political and industrial reform. Many of the rights we now take for granted we owe to people such as them.

ROMILEY, *Sandy Lane c1950* R255017

In the one hundred years following the building of the Peak Forest Canal in 1801 the population of Romiley tripled. This quiet residential road is very close to the centre of the town, yet even that fact has not saved the cinema on the left from demolition. The site has now been used for the building of a block of flats.

MARPLE BRIDGE
Town Street c1950
M156009

The bridge that gives the town its name is just off to the right of the photograph. It is not known when the first bridge was built; we just know that the bridge built in 1621 replaced an earlier one. The River Goyt, which brings water down from the hills, can be very turbulent at times, and it is known that at least one bridge has been washed away.

MARPLE BRIDGE
The Village c1955
M156008

Today Marple Bridge is the most delightfully pretty little village. In 1788, however, it and its near neighbour Marple were transformed into centres of industry when Samuel Oldknow built a mill here employing 400 people. He also built roads and a chapel, so that when later there was severe unrest amongst mill workers in nearby towns, he remained highly respected by his own workers.

MARPLE BRIDGE
The Mill and the Canal c1965 M156020

The canal pictured here is the Peak Forest Canal, completed in 1801. Additional locks were added in 1805, and it was probably the building of these that caused near bankruptcy to Oldknow - he had to be rescued financially by Richard Arkwright. This warehouse was later used by a plastics factory; it then fell into disuse, until it was restored in 1976 and converted to offices.

DISLEY
Buxton Old Road
c1965 D154014

The original settlement of Disley was based along this, once presumably very dusty, road – the town's name is thought to come from an Old English word meaning 'dusty'. Then, in 1724, the first turnpiked route linking Manchester and London was built through Disley following the line of the Goyt River, and the focus of the settlement changed.

DISLEY, *Market Street c1965* D154009

This view shows the turnpiked road as it looks today. When the canal was built and linked the town with Manchester, new industries soon followed. Most of the mills built here were for cotton spinning and weaving; so many were established in the locality that just across the border in Derbyshire there is even a town called New Mills.

HANDFORTH
The Greyhound Inn and High Street c1965
H322020

Situated right on the border with what is now Greater Manchester, this was to become an extremely busy route for commuters travelling daily into the city. Fortunately, there is now a bypass around both Handforth and Wilmslow restoring relative peace to the area.

WILMSLOW, *Bank Square Gardens c1955* W103007

Once referred to as 'the largest village in England', Wilmslow also became an industrial centre in the 18th century. It was famous for the production of button moulding, although, as in so many towns in the area, cotton was also produced here. The bank (centre) that presumably gave the Square its name still survives, although most of the building has been converted into a pub.

WILMSLOW
Grove Street c1955
W103006

J E Johnson & Sons, whose advertisement can be seen on the right, was a business that was started in the 1800s by John Edward Johnson. He was a saddler and harness maker. In the early 1900s he and his sons produced and repaired bicycles, and later, like so many such businesses, they progressed to working with cars.

ALDERLEY EDGE
Chapel Road c1955
A29011

The spire of St Philip's Church is 175 feet tall, and has been described as 'the most graceful and best proportioned in Cheshire'. The church itself dates from 1852, a period when the town was just beginning to develop as an up-market residential area serving Manchester – a description that still aptly fits Alderley Edge. The shop on the corner (right) was also the village post office at one time.

ALDERLEY EDGE, *The Wizard c1955* A29024

The Edge was famous for its copper mines, so that this pub was originally called the Miners' Arms. When, at the beginning of the 20th century, the pub lost its licence, it then (believe it or not) became a temperance house! Its present name recalls a legend which says that King Arthur and his knights are sleeping in a cave somewhere here, looked after by Merlin.

ALDERLEY EDGE, *The Wizard's Well c1955* A29016

'Drink of this and take thy fill

For the water falls by the Wizard's will'.

Since the Edge was close to Manchester by rail, excursions here became extremely popular in the late 19th century. Before long it had become the custom for a girl who was seeking a husband to throw a bent pin into the well for good luck in her search.

ALDERLEY EDGE
Stormy Point
c1955 A29021

This viewpoint is some 600 feet above sea level, and gives magnificent views into Derbyshire – and some say, as far as Yorkshire. Cracks in the rocks near here are the entrances to old mines; most of the caverns below have been sealed, but some are still accessible for cavers. The whole area is still popular with visitors, and has been maintained by the National Trust since 1947.

NETHER ALDERLEY
The Village Post Office
c1955 N148006

Both now privately owned houses, the building on the right was the village shop and post office, whilst the black and white building was once a pub, the Eagle and Child, more popularly known amongst the locals as the Bird and Babby. The eagle and child is the crest of the Stanley family.

CHELFORD, *The Village c1955* C461016

Once a common sight throughout the country, roadside petrol pumps such as those shown here are a severe fire risk, and are now placed well away from the kerb. The bridge just beyond the pumps goes over the railway line; this was the scene in 1894 of a terrible rail accident resulting in 14 deaths when an express train ran into a wagon that was being shunted here.

PRESTBURY
The Village c1955 P111011

Said to be the 'wealthiest parochial area' in Britain, Prestbury is now stockbroker country. The magpie building in the centre here is now the National Westminster Bank – when the photograph is enlarged, a sign is visible which reads 'District Bank'. It is known as the Priest's House, and was built in the 1580s by Thomas Legh. It became a bank in the 1920s.

BOLLINGTON, *General View c1955* B519006

This photograph looks down on the town from an aqueduct along the Macclesfield Canal, the last canal to be built in England, which opened in 1831. It was built to transport cotton and silk as well as coal and stone; today, used mainly by holidaymakers, it is considered one of the prettiest waterways in the country.

BOLLINGTON
Church Street c1955
B519040

'A thriving village with some collieries and extensive cotton factories' was how Bollington was described in 1848. Those factories were especially renowned for the quality of their Liberty cottons. Recent road schemes have meant that the mill-workers' cottages on the right have been demolished to make way for a new roundabout, with a modern block of flats instead.

MACCLESFIELD
Market Place c1955
M2017

Macclesfield became a borough in 1220, and by the17th century it was described as 'one of the fairest towns in Cheshire'. The market that was traditionally held here was moved away in 1973, but it was recently brought back for a trial period after a campaign by local traders. The Town Hall, on the left, was built in 1823-24.

MACCLESFIELD
Mill Street c1955
M2016

Mill Street was so named because it was at the bottom of this street in 1743 that Charles Roe established his silk mill (not visible here). Previously, silk production had been very much a cottage industry, but by the middle of the 18th century, mills powered at first by water and then by steam changed everything.

GAWSWORTH, *The Church and the Rectory c1955* G5015

The rectory was built in 1707. Inside there is a Jacobean chimneypiece that originally came from Pershore in Worcestershire. Behind the rectory, St James' Church is unusual in that it has a very wide nave and no aisles. It dates from the 15th century, but it was 'severely' restored in 1851.

GAWSWORTH
The Village c1955
G5022

In the heart of the village, close to this spot, lies Maggoty's Wood, where Maggoty Johnson was buried in 1773. He was the last paid court jester in England, and lived at the nearby Old Hall. There the tradition for entertainment continues, as it is now the superb setting for annual summer outdoor concerts and plays.

LANGLEY, *Ridgegate Reservoir c1955* L309006

Situated on the edge of the Macclesfield Forest, the Ridgegate Reservoir was one of the first reservoirs built to supply local towns. It was constructed in 1850, and as demand outstripped supply, others followed in 1871 and then in 1929. Today the Ridgegate Treatment Works can process 2 million gallons of water each day. The forest all around is also a wonderful recreation area.

WILDBOARCLOUGH
Crag Bridge c1960
W369008

It looks innocent enough in this view, but the Clough Brook has been known to cause serious damage when in flood. The most recent occasion was in 1989, when damage worth millions of pounds was caused by flooding; the bridge here was destroyed, and has since been restored. The name Wildboarclough has nothing to do with animals – it means 'the wild stream in the valley.

BOSLEY, *The Reservoir and the Cloud c1955* B108003

Beyond Bosley Reservoir, the Cloud is the name given to the hill in the distance. It rises to a height of 1125 feet, and from the top it is possible to see right across the Cheshire Plain towards Wales. There is a tradition that each Good Friday there is a walk here. Today the land is managed by the National Trust.

TIMBERSBROOK
The View from Cloud Road
c1955 T219006

Actually, it is not necessary to climb to the top of the Cloud to get an excellent view across Cheshire. This is the view from the road on the western side of the hill. The viaduct in the centre of the picture is for the railway line linking Macclesfield and Congleton.

CONGLETON, *High Street c1955* C151038

Although Congleton produced the most silk of the two towns, for some reason it was always Macclesfield further north that was known as 'the silk town' – but ribbons (nylon ones these days) are still produced in Congleton. Looking at these old Frith photographs, I am struck by the presence of so many blinds outside shops on sunny days – you never seem to see these today.

CONGLETON
Bridge Street c1955
C151035

The first English branch of Woolworth's was opened in Liverpool in 1909, and before long there was a branch of F W Woolworth on virtually every high street in the country; but many have disappeared in recent years. The branch shown here (right) has been replaced by a branch of Superdrug. The buildings just beyond have been pulled down and replaced.

113

ASTBURY, *The Church c1955* A215024

One of the finest churches in Cheshire, St Mary's has a lovely setting overlooking the village green. This picture gives some indication of its style, with its tower and spire almost totally separated from the main body of the church. The interior is superb, despite damage done by Roundhead soldiers who stabled their horses here during the time of the Civil War.

INDEX

Acton Bridge 70

Alderley Edge 102, 103, 104-105

Allostock 73

Alsager 91

Altrincham 55

Astbury 114

Aston-by-Sutton 42

Barnton 10, 71

Bebington 18

Beeston 83

Birkenhead 14-15, 16-17

Bollington 106

Bosley 110

Bunbury 85

Burton 26-27

Chelford 105

Chester 32-33, 34-35, 36-37

Church Minshull 88

Comberbach 71

Congleton 111, 112-113

Crewe 88, 89

Daresbury 42

Davenham 67

Delamere 62-63

Disley 98

Dunham Massey 54

Eaton 82

Eccleston 37

Ellesmere Port 12, 30, 31

Farndon 38

Frodsham 59, 60-61

Gawsworth 108, 109

Goostrey 74-75, 76-77

Grappenhall 50, 51

Great Budworth 72

Handforth 99

Hartford 67

Haslington 90

Hatchmere 60, 61

Helsby 58, 59

Heswall 21, 22

High Legh 52

Higher Walton 44

Holmes Chapel 76

Hooton 30

Hoylake 20, 21

Hyde 92-93, 94-95

Knutsford 52-53

Langley 109

Little Budworth 64-65

Lower Peover 72-73

Lymm 51

Macclesfield 106-107

Marple Bridge 96-97

Middlewich 77

Mobberley 53, 54-55

Mollington 31

Moore 43

Nantwich 86, 87

Neston 22-23

Nether Alderley 104

Northwich 68-69

Over 78

Parkgate 24-25

Peckforton 84

Prestbury 105

Puddington 27

Romiley 96

Runcorn 41

Sale 56, 57

Sandbach 90-91

Sandiway 66

Tarporley 81, 82-83

Thelwall 50-51

Timbersbrook 111

Upton 18-19

Warrington 44-45, 46-47, 48

Weaverham 69, 70

Wharton 78

Whitegate 66

Widnes 39, 40-41

Wildboarclough 110

Willaston 27, 28-29

Wilmslow 99, 100-101

Winsford 78-79, 80

Winwick 48

Wistaston 87

Woolston 49

Wrenbury 86-87

Frith Book Co Titles

www.francisfrith.co.uk

The Frith Book Company publishes over 100 new titles each year. A selection of those currently available is listed below. For latest catalogue please contact Frith Book Co.
Town Books 96 pages, approximately 100 photos. **County and Themed Books** 128 pages, approximately 150 photos (unless specified). All titles hardback with laminated case and jacket, except those indicated pb (paperback)

Amersham, Chesham & Rickmansworth (pb)	1-85937-340-2	£9.99	Derbyshire Living Memories	1-85937-330-5	£14.99
Andover (pb)	1-85937-292-9	£9.99	Devon (pb)	1-85937-297-x	£9.99
Aylesbury (pb)	1-85937-227-9	£9.99	Devon Churches (pb)	1-85937-250-3	£9.99
Barnstaple (pb)	1-85937-300-3	£9.99	Dorchester (pb)	1-85937-307-0	£9.99
Basildon Living Memories (pb)	1-85937-515-4	£9.99	Dorset (pb)	1-85937-269-4	£9.99
Bath (pb)	1-85937-419-0	£9.99	Dorset Coast (pb)	1-85937-299-6	£9.99
Bedford (pb)	1-85937-205-8	£9.99	Dorset Living Memories (pb)	1-85937-584-7	£9.99
Bedfordshire Living Memories	1-85937-513-8	£14.99	Down the Severn (pb)	1-85937-560-x	£9.99
Belfast (pb)	1-85937-303-8	£9.99	Down The Thames (pb)	1-85937-278-3	£9.99
Berkshire (pb)	1-85937-191-4	£9.99	Down the Trent	1-85937-311-9	£14.99
Berkshire Churches	1-85937-170-1	£17.99	East Anglia (pb)	1-85937-265-1	£9.99
Berkshire Living Memories	1-85937-332-1	£14.99	East Grinstead (pb)	1-85937-138-8	£9.99
Black Country	1-85937-497-2	£12.99	East London	1-85937-080-2	£14.99
Blackpool (pb)	1-85937-393-3	£9.99	East Sussex (ph)	1-85937-606-1	£9.99
Bognor Regis (pb)	1-85937-431-x	£9.99	Eastbourne (pb)	1-85937-399-2	£9.99
Bournemouth (pb)	1-85937-545-6	£9.99	Edinburgh (pb)	1-85937-193-0	£8.99
Bradford (pb)	1-85937-204-x	£9.99	England In The 1880s	1-85937-331-3	£17.99
Bridgend (pb)	1-85937-386-0	£7.99	Essex - Second Selection	1-85937-456-5	£14.99
Bridgwater (pb)	1-85937-305-4	£9.99	Essex (pb)	1-85937-270-8	£9.99
Bridport (pb)	1-85937-327-5	£9.99	Essex Coast	1-85937-342-9	£14.99
Brighton (pb)	1-85937-192-2	£8.99	Essex Living Memories	1-85937-490-5	£14.99
Bristol (pb)	1-85937-264-3	£9.99	Exeter	1-85937-539-1	£9.99
British Life A Century Ago (pb)	1-85937-213-9	£9.99	Exmoor (pb)	1-85937-608-8	£9.99
Buckinghamshire (pb)	1-85937-200-7	£9.99	Falmouth (pb)	1-85937-594-4	£9.99
Camberley (pb)	1-85937-222-8	£9.99	Folkestone (pb)	1-85937-124-8	£9.99
Cambridge (pb)	1-85937-422-0	£9.99	Frome (pb)	1-85937-317-8	£9.99
Cambridgeshire (pb)	1-85937-420-4	£9.99	Glamorgan	1-85937-488-3	£14.99
Cambridgeshire Villages	1-85937-523-5	£14.99	Glasgow (pb)	1-85937-190-6	£9.99
Canals And Waterways (pb)	1-85937-291-0	£9.99	Glastonbury (pb)	1-85937-338-0	£7.99
Canterbury Cathedral (pb)	1-85937-179-5	£9.99	Gloucester (pb)	1-85937-232-5	£9.99
Cardiff (pb)	1-85937-093-4	£9.99	Gloucestershire (pb)	1-85937-561-8	£9.99
Carmarthenshire (pb)	1-85937-604-5	£9.99	Great Yarmouth (pb)	1-85937-426-3	£9.99
Chelmsford (pb)	1-85937-310-0	£9.99	Greater Manchester (pb)	1-85937-266-x	£9.99
Cheltenham (pb)	1-85937-095-0	£9.99	Guildford (pb)	1-85937-410-7	£9.99
Cheshire (pb)	1-85937-271-6	£9.99	Hampshire (pb)	1-85937-279-1	£9.99
Chester (pb)	1-85937-382 8	£9.99	Harrogate (pb)	1-85937-423-9	£9.99
Chesterfield (pb)	1-85937-378-x	£9.99	Hastings and Bexhill (pb)	1-85937-131-0	£9.99
Chichester (pb)	1-85937-228-7	£9.99	Heart of Lancashire (pb)	1-85937-197-3	£9.99
Churches of East Cornwall (pb)	1-85937-249-x	£9.99	Helston (pb)	1-85937-214-7	£9.99
Churches of Hampshire (pb)	1-85937-207-4	£9.99	Hereford (pb)	1-85937-175-2	£9.99
Cinque Ports & Two Ancient Towns	1-85937-492-1	£14.99	Herefordshire (pb)	1-85937-567-7	£9.99
Colchester (pb)	1-85937-188-4	£8.99	Herefordshire Living Memories	1-85937-514-6	£14.99
Cornwall (pb)	1-85937-229-5	£9.99	Hertfordshire (pb)	1-85937-247-3	£9.99
Cornwall Living Memories	1-85937-248-1	£14.99	Horsham (pb)	1-85937-432-8	£9.00
Cotswolds (pb)	1-85937-230-9	£9.99	Humberside (pb)	1-85937-605-3	£9.99
Cotswolds Living Memories	1-85937-255-4	£14.99	Hythe, Romney Marsh, Ashford (pb)	1-85937-256-2	£9.99
County Durham (pb)	1-85937-398-4	£9.99	Ipswich (pb)	1-85937-424-7	£9.99
Croydon Living Memories (pb)	1-85937-162-0	£9.99	Isle of Man (pb)	1-85937-268-6	£9.99
Cumbria (pb)	1-85937-621-5	£9.99	Isle of Wight (pb)	1-85937-429-8	£9.99
Derby (pb)	1-85937-367-4	£9.99	Isle of Wight Living Memories	1-85937-304-6	£14.99
Derbyshire (pb)	1-85937-196-5	£9.99	Kent (pb)	1-85937-189-2	£9.99

Available from your local bookshop or from the publisher

Frith Book Co Titles (continued)

Lake District (pb)	1-85937-275-9	£9.99	Sherborne (pb)	1-85937-301-1	£9.99
Lancashire Living Memories	1-85937-335-6	£14.99	Shrewsbury (pb)	1-85937-325-9	£9.99
Lancaster, Morecambe, Heysham (pb)	1-85937-233-3	£9.99	Shropshire (pb)	1-85937-326-7	£9.99
Leeds (pb)	1-85937-202-3	£9.99	Shropshire Living Memories	1-85937-643-6	£14.99
Leicester (pb)	1-85937-381-x	£9.99	Somerset	1-85937-153-1	£14.99
Leicestershire & Rutland Living Memories	1-85937-500-6	£12.99	South Devon Coast	1-85937-107-8	£14.99
Leicestershire (pb)	1-85937-185-x	£9.99	South Devon Living Memories (pb)	1-85937-609-6	£9.99
Lighthouses	1-85937-257-0	£9.99	South East London (pb)	1-85937-263-5	£9.99
Lincoln (pb)	1-85937-380-1	£9.99	South Somerset	1-85937-318-6	£14.99
Lincolnshire (pb)	1-85937-433-6	£9.99	South Wales	1-85937-519-7	£14.99
Liverpool and Merseyside (pb)	1-85937-234-1	£9.99	Southampton (pb)	1-85937-427-1	£9.99
London (pb)	1-85937-183-3	£9.99	Southend (pb)	1-85937-313-5	£9.99
London Living Memories	1-85937-454-9	£14.99	Southport (pb)	1-85937-425-5	£9.99
Ludlow (pb)	1-85937-176-0	£9.99	St Albans (pb)	1-85937-341-0	£9.99
Luton (pb)	1-85937-235-x	£9.99	St Ives (pb)	1-85937-415-8	£9.99
Maidenhead (pb)	1-85937-339-9	£9.99	Stafford Living Memories (pb)	1-85937-503-0	£9.99
Maidstone (pb)	1-85937-391-7	£9.99	Staffordshire (pb)	1-85937-308-9	£9.99
Manchester (pb)	1-85937-198-1	£9.99	Stourbridge (pb)	1-85937-530-8	£9.99
Marlborough (pb)	1-85937-336-4	£9.99	Stratford upon Avon (pb)	1-85937-388-7	£9.99
Middlesex	1-85937-158-2	£14.99	Suffolk (pb)	1-85937-221-x	£9.99
Monmouthshire	1-85937-532-4	£14.99	Suffolk Coast (pb)	1-85937-610-x	£9.99
New Forest (pb)	1-85937-390-9	£9.99	Surrey (pb)	1-85937-240-6	£9.99
Newark (pb)	1-85937-366-6	£9.99	Surrey Living Memories	1-85937-328-3	£14.99
Newport, Wales (pb)	1-85937-258-9	£9.99	Sussex (pb)	1-85937-184-1	£9.99
Newquay (pb)	1-85937-421-2	£9.99	Sutton (pb)	1-85937-337-2	£9.99
Norfolk (pb)	1-85937-195-7	£9.99	Swansea (pb)	1-85937-167-1	£9.99
Norfolk Broads	1-85937-486-7	£14.99	Taunton (pb)	1-85937-314-3	£9.99
Norfolk Living Memories (pb)	1-85937-402-6	£9.99	Tees Valley & Cleveland (pb)	1-85937-623-1	£9.99
North Buckinghamshire	1-85937-626-6	£14.99	Teignmouth (pb)	1-85937-370-4	£7.99
North Devon Living Memories	1-85937-261-9	£14.99	Thanet (pb)	1-85937-116-7	£9.99
North Hertfordshire	1-85937-547-2	£14.99	Tiverton (pb)	1-85937-178-7	£9.99
North London (pb)	1-85937-403-4	£9.99	Torbay (pb)	1-85937-597-9	£9.99
North Somerset	1-85937-302-x	£14.99	Truro (pb)	1-85937-598-7	£9.99
North Wales (pb)	1-85937-298-8	£9.99	Victorian & Edwardian Dorset	1-85937-254-6	£14.99
North Yorkshire (pb)	1-85937-236-8	£9.99	Victorian & Edwardian Kent (pb)	1-85937-624-X	£9.99
Northamptonshire Living Memories	1-85937-529-4	£14.99	Victorian & Edwardian Maritime Album (pb)	1-85937-622-3	£9.99
Northamptonshire	1-85937-150-7	£14.99	Victorian and Edwardian Sussex (pb)	1-85937-625-8	£9.99
Northumberland Tyne & Wear (pb)	1-85937-281-3	£9.99	Villages of Devon (pb)	1-85937-293-7	£9.99
Northumberland	1-85937-522-7	£14.99	Villages of Kent (pb)	1-85937-294-5	£9.99
Norwich (pb)	1-85937-194-9	£8.99	Villages of Sussex (pb)	1-85937-295-3	£9.99
Nottingham (pb)	1-85937-324-0	£9.99	Warrington (pb)	1-85937-507-3	£9.99
Nottinghamshire (pb)	1-85937-187-6	£9.99	Warwick (pb)	1-85937-518-9	£9.99
Oxford (pb)	1-85937-411-5	£9.99	Warwickshire (pb)	1-85937-203-1	£9.99
Oxfordshire (pb)	1-85937-430-1	£9.99	Welsh Castles (pb)	1-85937-322-4	£9.99
Oxfordshire Living Memories	1-85937-525-1	£14.99	West Midlands (pb)	1-85937-289-9	£9.99
Paignton (pb)	1-85937-374-7	£7.99	West Sussex (pb)	1-85937-607-x	£9.99
Peak District (pb)	1-85937-280-5	£9.99	West Yorkshire (pb)	1-85937-201-5	£9.99
Pembrokeshire	1-85937-262-7	£14.99	Weston Super Mare (pb)	1-85937-306-2	£9.99
Penzance (pb)	1-85937-595-2	£9.99	Weymouth (pb)	1-85937-209-0	£9.99
Peterborough (pb)	1-85937-219-8	£9.99	Wiltshire (pb)	1-85937-277-5	£9.99
Picturesque Harbours	1-85937-208-2	£14.99	Wiltshire Churches (pb)	1-85937-171-x	£9.99
Piers	1-85937-237-6	£17.99	Wiltshire Living Memories (pb)	1-85937-396-8	£9.99
Plymouth (pb)	1-85937-389-5	£9.99	Winchester (pb)	1-85937-428-x	£9.99
Poole & Sandbanks (pb)	1-85937-251-1	£9.99	Windsor (pb)	1-85937-333-x	£9.99
Preston (pb)	1-85937-212-0	£9.99	Wokingham & Bracknell (pb)	1-85937-329-1	£9.99
Reading (pb)	1-85937-238-4	£9.99	Woodbridge (pb)	1-85937-498-0	£9.99
Redhill to Reigate (pb)	1-85937-596-0	£9.99	Worcester (pb)	1-85937-165-5	£9.99
Ringwood (pb)	1-85937-384-4	£7.99	Worcestershire Living Memories	1-85937-489-1	£14.99
Romford (pb)	1-85937-319-4	£9.99	Worcestershire	1-85937-152-3	£14.99
Royal Tunbridge Wells (pb)	1-85937-504-9	£9.99	York (pb)	1-85937-199-x	£9.99
Salisbury (pb)	1-85937-239-2	£9.99	Yorkshire (pb)	1-85937-186-8	£9.99
Scarborough (pb)	1-85937-379-8	£9.99	Yorkshire Coastal Memories	1-85937-506-5	£14.99
Sevenoaks and Tonbridge (pb)	1-85937-392-5	£9.99	Yorkshire Dales	1-85937-502-2	£14.99
Sheffield & South Yorks (pb)	1-85937-267-8	£9.99	Yorkshire Living Memories (pb)	1-85937-397-6	£9.99

See Frith books on the internet at www.francisfrith.co.uk

FRITH PRODUCTS & SERVICES

Francis Frith would doubtless be pleased to know that the pioneering publishing venture he started in 1860 still continues today. Over a hundred and forty years later, The Francis Frith Collection continues in the same innovative tradition and is now one of the foremost publishers of vintage photographs in the world. Some of the current activities include:

Interior Decoration

Today Frith's photographs can be seen framed and as giant wall murals in thousands of pubs, restaurants, hotels, banks, retail stores and other public buildings throughout the country. In every case they enhance the unique local atmosphere of the places they depict and provide reminders of gentler days in an increasingly busy and frenetic world.

Product Promotions

Frith products are used by many major companies to promote the sales of their own products or to reinforce their own history and heritage. Frith promotions have been used by Hovis bread, Courage beers, Scots Porage Oats, Colman's mustard, Cadbury's foods, Mellow Birds coffee, Dunhill pipe tobacco, Guinness, and Bulmer's Cider.

Genealogy and Family History

As the interest in family history and roots grows world-wide, more and more people are turning to Frith's photographs of Great Britain for images of the towns, villages and streets where their ancestors lived; and, of course, photographs of the churches and chapels where their ancestors were christened, married and buried are an essential part of every genealogy tree and family album.

Frith Products

All Frith photographs are available Framed or just as Mounted Prints and Posters (size 23 x 16 inches). These may be ordered from the address below. From time to time other products - Address Books, Calendars, Table Mats, etc - are available.

The Internet

Already fifty thousand Frith photographs can be viewed and purchased on the internet through the Frith websites and a myriad of partner sites.

For more detailed information on Frith companies and products, look at these sites:

www.francisfrith.co.uk
www.francisfrith.com
(for North American visitors)

See the complete list of Frith Books at:

www.francisfrith.co.uk

This web site is regularly updated with the latest list of publications from the Frith Book Company. If you wish to buy books relating to another part of the country that your local bookshop does not stock, you may purchase on-line.

For further information, trade, or author enquiries please contact us at the address below:
The Francis Frith Collection, Frith's Barn, Teffont, Salisbury, Wiltshire, England SP3 5QP.
Tel: +44 (0)1722 716 376   Fax: +44 (0)1722 716 881   Email: sales@francisfrith.co.uk

See Frith books on the internet at www.francisfrith.co.uk

FREE MOUNTED PRINT

Mounted Print
Overall size 14 x 11 inches

Fill in and cut out this voucher and return
it with your remittance for £2.25 (to cover postage and handling). Offer valid for delivery to UK addresses only.

Choose any photograph included in this book.
Your SEPIA print will be A4 in size. It will be mounted in a cream mount with a burgundy rule line (overall size 14 x 11 inches).

**Order additional Mounted Prints
at HALF PRICE (only £7.49 each*)**
If you would like to order more Frith prints from this book, possibly as gifts for friends and family, you can buy them at half price (with no additional postage and handling costs).

Have your Mounted Prints framed
For an extra £14.95 per print* you can have your mounted print(s) framed in an elegant polished wood and gilt moulding, overall size 16 x 13 inches (no additional postage and handling required).

---

* IMPORTANT!

These special prices are only available if you order at the same time as you order your free mounted print. You must use the ORIGINAL VOUCHER on this page (no copies permitted). We can only despatch to one address.

Send completed Voucher form to:
The Francis Frith Collection, Frith's Barn, Teffont, Salisbury, Wiltshire SP3 5QP

Voucher **for FREE** *and Reduced Price Frith Prints*

Please do not photocopy this voucher. Only the original is valid, so please fill it in, cut it out and return it to us with your order.

Picture ref no	Page no	Qty	Mounted @ £7.49	Framed + £14.95	Total Cost
		1	Free of charge*	£	£
			£7.49	£	£
			£7.49	£	£
			£7.49	£	£
			£7.49	£	£
			£7.49	£	£
Please allow 28 days for delivery			* Post & handling (UK)		£2.25
			Total Order Cost		£

Title of this book . . . .

I enclose a cheque/postal order for £ . . . .
made payable to 'The Francis Frith Collection'

OR please debit my Mastercard / Visa / Switch / Amex card
(credit cards please on all overseas orders), details below

Card Number

Issue No (Switch only)　　　　Valid from (Amex/Switch)

Expires　　　　　　Signature

Name Mr/Mrs/Ms . . . .

Address . . . .

. . . .

. . . .

. . . . Postcode . . . .

Daytime Tel No . . . .

Email . . . .

Valid to 31/12/05

Would you like to find out more about Francis Frith?

We have recently recruited some entertaining speakers who are happy to visit local groups, clubs and societies to give an illustrated talk documenting Frith's travels and photographs. If you are a member of such a group and are interested in hosting a presentation, we would love to hear from you.

Our speakers bring with them a small selection of our local town and county books, together with sample prints. They are happy to take orders. A small proportion of the order value is donated to the group who have hosted the presentation. The talks are therefore an excellent way of fundraising for small groups and societies.

Can you help us with information about any of the Frith photographs in this book?

We are gradually compiling an historical record for each of the photographs in the Frith archive. It is always fascinating to find out the names of the people shown in the pictures, as well as insights into the shops, buildings and other features depicted.

If you recognize anyone in the photographs in this book, or if you have information not already included in the author's caption, do let us know. We would love to hear from you, and will try to publish it in future books or articles.

Our production team

Frith books are produced by a small dedicated team at offices in the converted Grade II listed 18th-century barn at Teffont near Salisbury, illustrated above. Most have worked with the Frith Collection for many years. All have in common one quality: they have a passion for the Frith Collection. The team is constantly expanding, but currently includes:

Paul Baron, Jason Buck, John Buck, Ruth Butler, Heather Crisp, David Davies, Isobel Hall, Julian Hight, Peter Horne, James Kinnear, Karen Kinnear, Tina Leary, Stuart Login, David Marsh, Sue Molloy, Glenda Morgan, Wayne Morgan, Kate Rotondetto, Dean Scource, Eliza Sackett, Terence Sackett, Sandra Sampson, Adrian Sanders, Sandra Sanger, Julia Skinner, Claire Tarrier, Lewis Taylor, Shelley Tolcher, Lorraine Tuck and Jeremy Walker.